MADE TO THRIVE

THE CHAMPION'S DIET

Margaret Njuguna

WESTBOW
PRESS®
A DIVISION OF THOMAS NELSON
& ZONDERVAN

WestBow Press books may be ordered through booksellers or by contacting:

WestBow Press
A Division of Thomas Nelson & Zondervan
1663 Liberty Drive
Bloomington, IN 47403
www.westbowpress.com
844-714-3454

Scriptures taken from the Holy Bible, New International Version®, NIV®. Copyright © 1973, 1978, 1984, 2011 by Biblica, Inc.™ Used by permission of Zondervan. All rights reserved worldwide. www.zondervan. com The "NIV" and "New International Version" are trademarks registered in the United States Patent and Trademark Office by Biblica, Inc.®

ISBN: 978-1-6642-4792-5 (sc)
ISBN: 978-1-6642-4794-9 (hc)
ISBN: 978-1-6642-4793-2 (e)

Library of Congress Control Number: 2021921492

Print information available on the last page.

WestBow Press rev. date: 11/09/2021

It is with much pleasure that I endorse *Made to Thrive* by Pastor Margaret. I have had the honor of serving under Pastor James and Pastor Margaret at TORIM Church for several years.

In her book, she challenged me to take a good look at my spiritual walk with her first question, "Are you surviving, thriving, or actually stagnant?"

The Lord has gifted Pastor Margaret with a gentle and loving spirit that enables her to point out problematic issues that can cause you to grow stagnant in your walk with God. Then with a passionate heart, she encourages you and lifts you back up onto the pathway of righteousness, giving godly solutions to thrive again!

This is a must-read book because no matter how long you have been serving or have known God, you can easily fall into the trap of the devil and become stagnant in your journey with the Lord. It is also possible to be stagnant in your career, marriage, or business, and through this book, you will understand how to reignite your fire and passion and pursue your dreams. When we are stagnant, it means we cannot be fruitful, which, as pastor Margaret has explained in detail, is an expectation in every level of our lives. When we are well connected with the true vine, it is easier to thrive both spiritually and physically.

Thank you, Pastor Margaret, for being obedient and writing such a great book.

Much love.

—Pastor Bertha Hanna, TORIM Church, El Paso Texas

The Bible refers to the believer as a tree of righteousness, the planting of the Lord. It is a key pointer that God is interested in the seed, the process, and the fruit. Jesus taught meticulously on Him being the true vine and the believers the branches designed to bear much fruit.

This great epistle by Pastor Margaret brings forth this powerful truth, albeit in a profound way. For any believer keen on having a progressive walk with the Lord and lasting fruit, *Made to Thrive* is a must-read.

Having encountered Reverend James Mutero and Pastor Margaret on and off pulpit, I can boldly testify this is an overflow of their own Christ-centered lives.

I recommend this book to anyone who has a mind of fulfilling purpose and accomplishing destiny. This is the champion's diet.

—Apostle Joe Butali, President and Founder, Eagles Gathering ministries, Nairobi, Kenya

Made to Thrive is a must-read for all who have purposed to pursue their purpose in life and are willing to arise even amid crisis and failure.

The book's main proposition clearly indicates that we all have a purpose that God created us for and expects us to pursue and achieve. It is through understanding our purpose that we can then seek the right strategies and resources to passionately and relentlessly work toward our destiny. Pastor Margaret has given you the critical keys on how to thrive in your spiritual and physical lives through this needed book, *Made to Thrive*. You will also be able to understand and evaluate your spiritual success and shed light on what thriving means in your life. *Made to Thrive* is a special book that will open your spiritual eye and your view on how to carry yourself spiritually, which will propel you to new dimensions.

Made to Thrive also has great product qualities, which will help you understand failure to thrive both physically and spiritually, its causes, and how to avoid or prevent it. This will lead to advancement and flourishment in your physical and spiritual lives. The author has also shared how God has helped her grow from one glory to another despite challenges, and it will be a great encouragement for you. After reading this book, you will realize the great potential that is in you and how you can unleash it to make a difference in your world as you pursue your destiny.

This powerful epistle will not only challenge you to arise and pursue what you were made for but will also add value to your life by giving you clear guidelines on how to overcome the hurdles on your path. Once you have understood it, walk in victory and add value to others by sharing and modelling it. One of the greatest hurdles is your mindset, which Pastor Margaret discusses, elaborating in detail how you can overcome it by setting your mindset right and possessing your thoughts for success. No one can rise above their mindset or vision. Keep reading, and your life will be transformed. At whatever stage you are in, you can overcome. Trust in God, seek Him, and pursue what He made you for. Just like Pastor Margaret has said, it is your time, and this is your book. Read, share, and keep on thriving.

—Pastor Nancy Karuingi, Christian Foundation
Fellowship (CFF), Nairobi, Kenya

To my two beautiful daughters, Joy Njuguna and Peace Njuguna. You are both trailblazers with a growth mindset, marked for greatness, and no forces of the enemy can stop you. You have shown me from an early age that you can passionately pursue and achieve your goals through continuous efforts. May you live purposeful lives, taking every opportunity given to you to discover new things and remembering that success is doing your best. Moreover, never forget you have been called to do exploits in the kingdom of God, to serve humanity and to be the light and blessing to your generations. Nations will come to your light and kings to the brightness of your dawn.

And to my late and treasured parents, Mr. and Mrs. Johnson Kuria. I am what I am today because of the godly counsel and right foundation that you gave me. You took me to the house of God at an early age, and what I learned and have continued to learn has helped shape my life. Mom, you told me when I was a little girl that I would make an excellent nurse since I loved to help everybody. Today, by God's grace, I am a seasoned RN, living a life of resilience, fulfillment, and fruitfulness. I love to serve because you showed me how and never despised the little things that I did when I was young. I love you, and as a family, we shall forever treasure and celebrate you both.

CONTENTS

FOREWORD

I first met Pastor Margaret and her husband, Reverend James Mutero, in 2005. Right from the word go, I knew that they had something unique because when they walked in where we met, everybody was carried away by their charisma. They illuminated the room with God's presence and joy. I have interacted with Pastor Margaret and her husband as friends and as my pastors. I can confidently say that she is a woman of principle. She values her relationship with God. It illuminates her face whenever she talks about God. It doesn't matter the situation, place, or audience. She has understood her position as a child of God and never shies off to confess her relationship with God to her colleagues, strangers, children, family, and even friends.

In matters of excellence, diligence, and commitment, I have seen them all wrapped up in one person—Pastor Margaret. She has been a challenge to many by the way she is committed to the service of God and humanity. She is a loving mother, wife, pastor, registered nurse, and an advocate for healthy living, both physically and spiritually. She goes miles just to ensure that the body of Christ remains intact and in line with the Word of God.

She has a burden to bring the body of Christ to realization that there is a purpose and a reason for every life. She always says that each life is unique and created for a purpose. Every human being alive has an opportunity for great exploits, excellence, and access to both innate and physical resources for thriving. Hence her debut book, *Made to Thrive*.

Made to Thrive is a great book for every person and especially every believer. There is no better person to author such an amazing book other than Pastor Margaret herself. She discovered early that she was called to serve God and humanity. She aligned her life with the Word of God and has lived a life of thriving both in the ministry and in her career as a registered nurse administrator. Pastor Margaret has learned the secret of honoring and respecting authority whether at home, church, or her place of work. This has earned respect and honor from the superiors at work. She has been allocated greater responsibilities and promotions because of her diligence, commitment, and hard work. As she said in *Made to Thrive*, "If you have a dream, you can live a passionate and purposeful life and become what you dreamt."

You can achieve whatever you dream of. Don't let any obstacle hinder you. Pastor Margaret has challenged many, especially two years ago when she went back to school, despite her busy schedule as a wife, mother, pastor, and nurse administrator. She completed her bachelor's degree and has other national professional certifications attached to her name. She understands that she was made to thrive, and she is living it.

I recommend her book to everyone—those looking for a role model, anyone searching for a return to the crossroads, and anyone desiring to know his or her purpose in life and how to take it to the next level. Just know you were made to thrive. It is your time, so arise and pursue it.

—Rufus Mutitu, MSHS, RN BSN, Praise and Worship Team leader, TORIM Church, El Paso, Texas

ACKNOWLEDGMENTS

I humbly acknowledge the Lord Almighty and the grace He has bestowed upon my life. I am privileged to be a vessel of honor in Your kingdom, and I will forever glorify You.

To my loving husband, Pastor James Mutero, senior pastor and founder of Times of Refreshing International Ministries, I truly appreciate your love, support, prayers, and input in seeing this noble project as successful. I honor God's grace in your life and will forever be grateful for the opportunity and honor of serving with you. We must remain relevant and useful in accomplishing God's end-time agenda. More grace and fresh anointing, dear, as the Lord continues to use you. You are a blessing to our generations.

My lovely daughters, Joy and Peace, I truly appreciate your support and encouragement throughout this project. When I thought I was spending way too much time on the book, you kept reminding me to keep writing. Thank you for understanding and loving my God. May you grow to love and serve Him with your generations. You are blessed and shall live to fulfil your days.

Archbishop Harrison Nganga, founder of CFF Churches, Kenya, thank you for giving my husband and me the right foundation in the ministry. For the eight years we sat under your authority, anointing teachings, and guidance, our lives changed. God used you to speak greatness in our lives, and we have seen God's faithfulness this far. I still remember in early 2000, I was a youth and had only five thousand Kenyan shillings. You were calling for people to come forward and contribute toward the hall payment. I brought the only money I had, and God used you to speak about me going to foreign countries. I can only say God is faithful. I love giving and will continue to serve God with gladness of heart. May the Lord multiply His grace upon your life and family, in Jesus's name.

Thank you to my friends and coworkers in ministry. Pastor Bertha Hanna, thank you for reminding me numerous times about God's grace to write books in my life and proofreading this book. I appreciate your invaluable input. Many blessings, dear. Bishop Margaret Wangari (ACF Banana, Kenya), I am honored to call you Mom and will forever be grateful to God for the divine connection. You came into my life when I desperately needed encouragement, prayer, support, and your wise counsel. Thank you for being there despite your busy schedule. I appreciate your guidance, Mom. Apostle Joe Butali (Eagles Gathering Church, Kenya), thank you for your support and endorsement. I appreciate your prayers, wisdom, and expertise. Prophet Caleb Wekesa (Balm of Gilead International Ministry, Kenya), thank you for faithfully communicating God's mind about this noble project even when you did not know me, and your continued prayers are much appreciated. Pastor Nancy Karuingi (CFF Nairobi, Kenya), I thank God for connecting us since our early days in ministry. I appreciate your love, prayers, and support. Thank you for endorsing this great epistle.

Brother Rufus Mutitu (TORIM Praise and Worship Team chairman), thank you for taking your time to proofread and edit my original manuscript. I appreciate you.

TORIM Church and Ministry members, you are a great part of my life, and I will be forever grateful to God for bringing you my way. May you live to love, laugh, humbly serve, and enjoy abundance in the kingdom of God as you pursue your purpose.

INTRODUCTION

Are You Thriving, Surviving, or Actually Stagnant?

> The righteous will flourish like a palm tree, they will grow like a cedar of Lebanon, planted in the house of the Lord, they will flourish in the courts of our God. They will still bear fruit in old age, and they will stay fresh and green.
>
> —Psalms 92:12–14 (NIV)

This Word clearly indicates that there is a connection between our walk with God, growth, and fruitfulness. Our God is a God of fruitfulness, and as long as we are in His will, we shall flourish and produce results through His divine power. It is God's will for every individual to prosper. His Word in Jeremiah 29:11 clearly states that He has good plans for each one of us, to prosper and to give us a future with a hope. The challenge is how much are we willing to pause, listen, and pursue God's will and purpose for us?

Your overflow in life is supposed to bring glory to God and make a difference in the lives of others around you. That is fruitfulness, which is an expectation from God.

- What have you heard or seen concerning your life?
- How desperate are you to bear fruits now, tomorrow, and every day?

May this book ignite a fresh fire in you that will propel you to the level the Lord predestined for you.

It is with great honor and humility that I would like to introduce this book to you and share with you a few words about my life and how the Lord has shifted me from one glory to another. I am still a work in progress and trusting God for more. He is a faithful God, and I will forever trust, serve, adore, and glorify Him.

My name is Margaret Njuguna. I am from Kenya. I was born and raised in a small village called Gathanga in Makuyu Division, Murang'a County. I was raised in the Anglican faith, where I gave my life to God as a young girl. I grew and served until I went to college in Nairobi and joined the Happy Church Ministry. It was during my growth path there that I learned about water baptism and decided to be immersed in water. This was not in line with the Anglican faith, and I had to inform my parents that I had been rebaptized. By God's grace, I was not punished for it, but my father insisted on knowing if I still believed in the Anglican faith. I will call that testimony for another day.

In 1997, I started visiting Archbishop Harrison Nganga's new church in Nairobi. The following year, I became one of his faithful members, where I continued to grow spiritually and served in the ministry. I met my husband, Pastor James Njuguna Mutero, in that church as we served together in praise and worship, choir, youth group, and leading church meetings. In December 2000, we were joined in holy matrimony by the bishop. We are blessed with two beautiful, God-fearing daughters who are a delight to have in the church and ministry.

My husband was ordained into full-time ministry in 2001. This was exactly eight months into our marriage, and although I was still figuring out how to be a wife, I had to quickly adjust to embrace the new role as a pastor's wife, supporting my husband, who was now serving full-time under Bishop Harrison while I continued with my nursing career. During the ordination, God spoke great things about the ministry that He had placed in our lives, which included ministering to people of different colors, and I knew it was imperative to commit myself to seek God and fully walk in His will and purpose. I must say it is only by God's grace that I was able to understand His plan and His strategies, which have kept me going this far.

Your prosperity is where God's voice is concerning you. You will succeed if you walk in the realm where that voice directs you and by His strategies. Seek to hear His voice and pursue His strategies in prayer. Moses stayed on the mountain with God, and that is where God gave him instructions for the Israelites. God called him to be a deliverer, but that was not enough; he needed to know how to do it. You may have heard the message from God, but you need His strategy to deliver or to reach there. Keep seeking God. Your purpose must be fulfilled in Him.

We relocated to Texas in 2006, where we are humbly serving God through Times of Refreshing International Ministries (TORIM). I must say serving God with my husband since 2001 has been a great joy despite the hurdles of ministry, and God has been faithful. It is not easy to have equilibrium as a pastor's wife, mother, nurse, and ministry, but through prayer, resilience, and embracing my purpose, I have experienced great joy and fulfillment in passionately serving God and humanity. By God's grace, I am dedicated to enriching lives with God's presence by supporting families, developing all ages spiritually, nurturing gifts, empowering women to arise to their rightful positions, and encouraging all to seek God and dig deeper to understand and become what they were made for. Additionally, I enjoy sharing health education with the community, and God has given me a great team that selflessly goes out of their way to educate, serve, and impact the world that God has placed us in. Through faith in God, I love and enjoy every step of my service to Him and humanity, and it is through these that I have continued to learn and evolve to the better version of what God made me be.

I am prayerfully looking forward to greater heights in works and possessions in my life and calling, and I know the Lord is faithful. Please trust Him with me, even for your life. He is faithful and just. He will do it. Position and blaze yourself for what you have envisioned. Pursue, and it will come to pass.

As you continue to read this book, evaluate yourself, identify where you are both physically and spiritually, possess your thoughts, intentionally plan, pray, get connected, and pursue. As long as you can see it, you are a candidate to achieve it in Jesus's name.

We are all at different levels and positions in our lives, both spiritually and physically. Let me remind you that where you are is a temporary position. The Lord's will for you and me is to be triumphant in our purposeful lives, but there are many enemies to conquer along the path of our success. The enemies of your destiny would like to keep you in a survival mode, where you are comfortably uncomfortable, so that you do not enjoy living passionately, fulfilling your purpose. Needless to mention, the stagnant spirit is a wild hurdle that ensures there is no advancement or fruitfulness in your life. This is a spirit we must vanquish because we were made to evolve from one glory to another. The Lord has expectations for each one of us at every level, and if we are not growing, then we cannot advance His kingdom and in our physical lives.

- Where are you in your life? Do you have a dream, a vision, or a purpose?

Whether you got your promotion yesterday, have been stagnant, or have been just surviving, this book is for you. A higher glory and possessions are awaiting. As you read this book, may the Lord open your eyes and ears to see and understand what He has for you. You have the potential to achieve it as long as you comply with God's will for you. Trust in His instructions, connect with the right resources and destiny helpers who will speak into your gift, arise, pursue, and recover all.

> And David inquired of the Lord, "Shall I pursue this raiding party? Will I overtake them?" "Pursue them," he answered. "You will certainly overtake them and succeed in the rescue." (1 Samuel 30:8 NIV)

Although David had lost everything, including his two wives, he did not just sit there in mourning. He knew something needed to happen, so he got up and inquired of the Lord, who he loved and trusted in. David knew his role and position were vital in seeing the change that he desired. You may have gone through fire, and it may seem like you have reached your end. Do not sit at the accident scene anymore. Arise, seek God, and connect with the help you need to rediscover yourself and change the game. You were built for it.

Have you seen what happens at an accident scene? The goal is always to clear the scene very fast to allow normalcy on the road. If those injured are left on the scene for a prolonged duration, their conditions may worsen, or they can even be reinjured by other motor vehicles and die. Arise from that scene in your thoughts and on your tongue and pursue what you were made for. Through this book, you will learn how to take possession of your thoughts, win the battles of your tongue, and become the version that God made and ordained.

Time for passive involvement in your growth path is over. Spring up, recharge the batteries of your faith, master your thoughts, speak it, and achieve it in Jesus's name. It is your time. Do not be passed by. Tell the Lord you are tired of failing, stagnation, survival, delays, and doing what everybody else is doing. He will show and direct you to the way out of it all; there is a way to your purpose. You are an influencer with great potential. It is not too late to activate it. Change and bless the world with the hidden and untapped gift and riches in you. Say bye to the old chapter; a new chapter is loading. Stay focused and enjoy it as you glorify God.

This book offers great tools, strength, hope, encouragement, and insights on how you can arise, shake off the dust, roll up your sleeves, and start living purposefully. Whether in your spiritual life, career, marriage, relationships, or finances, where fruitfulness is not evident anymore, God will guide you through this champion's diet, and you will start seeing positive changes, in Jesus's name. God's favor and instructions in your life require action, listening, understanding, and moving. It is time to defy all odds. Do not just exist or survive. Create time for what you want and live it. You were made to thrive!

CHAPTER 1
What Does Thriving Mean?

For us to understand and avoid the wrong rendition, we must meticulously attach the right and accurate meaning to words. I am sure you have heard about thriving many times, but it is my prayer that as you read this book, new interpretations and revelations will be spawned that will stretch your paradigms on success and prosperity, causing advancement in your life. To thrive is simply to have a notable success or flourish in well-being. It entails the bounty and progression in life that each one of us would like to be associated with.

Success is great, and we all want to be triumphant in every aspect of our lives. No one likes to be associated with failure. In other words, we all want to reach our full potential in life and achieve the purpose we were created for. The cause of our living produces potential in us that gives us the impetus to fight for our destiny. For us to prosper in our purpose, we must adhere to some disciplines and principles in our lives; otherwise, we end up being distracted and frustrated. Disastrously, most of us have not reached even half of our full potential, perhaps due to lack of understanding or failure to follow principles that should govern us. Violation of principles destroys purpose, and potential is not spared either. We shall explore those needful disciplines in this book so that you can learn how to employ them and overflow in your purpose.

Growth in the physical and spiritual realms involves a dynamic process that calls for work; it is not automatic or mechanical. When this lacks, then we all end up with what we are seeing today in our society—failure to thrive, which can be either physical or spiritual. The Bible gives a great illustration of a prosperous man by the simile of a tree both fruitful and flourishing. "That person is like a tree planted by streams of water, which yields its fruit in season and whose leaf does not wither and whatever they do prospers" (Psalm 1:3 NIV).

This is an admirable state to be in both in our physical and spiritual lives, but it calls for work and discipline.

According to the late Myles Monroe (a great leader, teacher, author, and minister in the kingdom of God), success is making it to the end of purpose. As you continue to read, you will see how much potential you have and what you need to do to reach your potential. You were made to be successful and must fight for it. God wants you to focus on your goals and attain them. Run your race to win it.

Understanding Failure to Thrive (FTT)

Being a registered nurse for more than twenty years, I have seen so many children at the hospitals with the diagnosis of failure to thrive (FTT). It is a real problem in our society. Many of us may not realize that they are suffering from it because it is not only a physical issue but also psychological, emotional, and spiritual. It is agonizing when a parent is given the diagnosis of failure to thrive, and many wonder what they are doing wrong in the care of their young ones. Every mother wants to see her baby thriving and going through every milestone normally. They would go any extra width and depth to see this achieved. All babies must be fed right to grow healthy and become strong and productive members of society. For this to happen, parents must practice needed and required disciplines to ensure presence, provision, and protection for their children. This includes physical, spiritual, emotional, and psychological nourishment; otherwise, stunted growth occurs.

According to Healthline (2019), "failure to thrive" describes a situation in which a child is undernourished and does not meet recognized standards of growth. The most common cause of failing to thrive is not taking in enough calories. Other risk factors that may contribute to poor nutrition include poor feeding habits, neglect, physical abuse, mental trauma, and mental health conditions, such as depression and poverty.

Since it can lead to permanent mental, emotional, and physical delays, it's important to have regular checkups so doctors can monitor the child's health. Failure to thrive that is not treated can result in long-term complications, including learning disabilities,

3

emotional problems, and restricted growth. Some cases of failure to thrive may be resolvable once a doctor treats the underlying condition. If failure to thrive requires further care, the child's doctor may prescribe nutritional supplements or a special diet based on the underlying diagnosis.

Failure to thrive is also seen in adults and happens when an older adult has a loss of appetite, eats and drinks less than usual, loses weight, and is less active than normal. He or she may not be interested in other people or social activities. He or she may also have memory loss, trouble thinking, and trouble with daily activities.

Just like in the physical, we also experience spiritual failure to thrive when our spirits are deprived of the right nutrients needed for spiritual growth. Spiritual failure to thrive can affect both young Christians and even those mature in faith if they stop feeding on the right nutrients and neglect their growth discipline. Billy Graham stated that "lack of growth in the Christian life is a tragedy and we must grow in the Grace and knowledge of Christ."

From the above explanation, it is very clear that growth is imperative in every stage and aspect of our lives, and this includes the spiritual and physical lives. Spiritually, we must take responsibility and intentionally create time to be fed, to grow, and to serve God as mature Christians. It is only when we are mature that we can be trusted to undertake great responsibilities in our areas of service. It is at this level that God trusts us with His missions, like Moses. He had grown to understand God's ways, and God trusted him. He spoke face-to-face with him and also trusted him with the hardest rescue mission for the Israelites.

In the corporate world, employers are searching for employees who are faithful, are honest, are open-minded, are ambitious to grow, can perform, can deliver results, and can positively influence and bring success to the company. You cannot be indolent at work or remain on preceptorship forever and expect to have a job tomorrow. There must be progressive and notable growth even when we are new hires. Furthermore, we all have to work hard to ensure we remain the stars in our companies for the employer to need us. This calls for hard work, self-discipline, and proving yourself to the employer that you are worthy of the position.

Sometime back, I was working as a charge nurse in a busy emergency room, and after about one year of hard work, I started feeling underutilized. I felt it was not a challenge anymore for me, and it had become a routine. I had worked so hard to educate and empower myself by doing extra courses and certifications. I had three national certifications and had connected with coaches from whom I learned a lot. Thus, the capacity within me had grown, and I needed more to do. I went to my director's office, and I was very honest about how I felt and asked her if she had something else I could do for the company. She was very appreciative of what I had done and was ready to mentor me in the next role. She offered me two options, and I chose to remain in ER and be the operations manager in an off-site emergency room, which was opening in a few months and was a new concept for the company. This was a great challenge, and I had to work hard to be influential out there and bring success in this new concept.

By God's grace, I excelled, and although it was challenging, it unveiled growth for me both in my career and ministry. If I had become too comfortable as a charge nurse, I could not have grown this far. I also had to identify my learning needs and create time to learn and become the best in it. Sometimes I had to hold educational meetings at five thirty in the morning for myself and others working under me. There are seasons in our lives that come to equip us, and we must be available.

I believe God also needs people who can discipline themselves to grow and keep on rising in His service. He is a God of order, and excellence is a heavenly language too. As you grow, God will honor your efforts, and you will succeed in your physical life too.

In a nutshell, growth is vital in every aspect of our lives, and results must be seen in both physical and spiritual aspects.

As you continue to read this book, you will understand your role in your own growth, which will help yield results. Moreover, you will understand what you can control in your life to help you grow and to continue seeing positive changes in your attitude, thoughts, and perspective. We must refuse to be part of the failure-to-thrive tragedy.

CHAPTER 2
Spiritual Thriving

When we become Christians, we enter into a relationship with God, Jesus, and the Holy Spirit that enhances our growth. With the power of the Holy Spirit, we are called to become more like Jesus and holier. Spiritual growth becomes a birthmark of our faith. According to the Bible, spiritual growth is moving from elementary teachings, which means there has to be advancement.

> Therefore, let us move beyond the elementary teachings about Christ and be taken forward to maturity, not laying again the foundation of repentance. (Hebrews 6:1 NIV)

This means that the growth process involves advancement from the infancy stage to understanding and maturity where fruitfulness is the result. As Christians, we must embrace the growth process and be disciplined to go through it to reach our full potential, just like in physical growth. The Lord expects there to be a continuous increasing of glory in our lives. This means that there must be a continuous progression into what we were made to be. This calls for us to be intentional about our spiritual growth and progress. We must create and invest time for God's Word, prayer, and corporate fellowship. Just like we are all committed to growing in the physical and can go any length to ensure we get what we are looking for, we must keep the discipline for our spiritual growth. In our relationship with God, we must be dynamic and allow the Holy Spirit to govern our spiritual affairs. Be careful of self-sufficiency; you cannot go too far alone. You will drown in the sea of stagnation. Allow the Holy Spirit, the Helper, to guide you.

> And we all, who with unveiled faces contemplate the Lord's glory, are being transformed into his image with ever-increasing glory, which comes from the Lord, who is the Spirit. (2 Corinthians 3:18 NIV)

Causes of Spiritual Failure to Thrive

Continuing in Secret Sin

Sin is a barrier that separates us from God and hence cuts the flow of the Holy Spirit in us, hindering our growth. We have to master our ways and confess our sins to God. He is faithful and just to forgive us. We should also observe the discipline of saying no to the enemy. If we want to grow, we must persist in doing what is right before God. This will keep us connected with Him, and we shall continue to thrive in our relationship with Him.

> But your iniquities have separated you from your God your sins have hidden his face from you so that he will not hear. (Isaiah 59:2 NIV)

We must resist the enemy as Jesus did. He went before us, and He overcame. Continued sin becomes an iniquity that can be passed to our generations. Refuse to be answerable to the failures of your generations by your sins.

> In your struggle against sin, you have not yet resisted to the point of shedding your blood. And have you completely forgotten this word of encouragement that addresses you as a father addresses his son? It says, "My son, do not make light of the Lord's discipline, and do not lose heart when he rebukes you, because the Lord disciplines the one, he loves, and he chastens everyone he accepts as his son." (Hebrews 12:4–6 NIV)

Growth is distinguishing good from evil and putting off the old self, which is corrupted by its deceitful desires. It is to put on a new self, created to be like God in righteousness and holiness. Also, it involves making new attitudes in our minds. Our faith is strengthened when we continually live in Christ, rooted and built up in Him.

Lack of Trust in God

Unbelief or feeling like the Lord is not in control hinders our growth in Him. Staying well connected and in fellowship with believers enhances our growth, leading to fruitfulness. This means as believers we must continually hear the Word of God, retain it, persevere, and develop faith in God. Learn to depend on God and the influence of His Holy Spirit.

> But the seed on good soil stands for those with a noble and good heart, who hear the word, retain it, and by persevering produce a crop. (Luke 8:15 NIV)

When we embrace and love the growth process, we become more stable in our faith in God and are not easily influenced by those outside the faith.

> Until we all reach unity in the faith and in the knowledge of the Son of God and become mature, attaining to the whole measure of the fullness of Christ. Then we will no longer be infants, tossed back and forth by the waves, and blown here and there by every wind of teaching and by the cunning and craftiness of people in their deceitful scheming. Instead, speaking the truth in love, we will grow to become in every respect the mature body of him who is the head, that is, Christ. (Ephesians 4:13–15 NIV)

Spiritual Malnutrition

Just like in the physical, when a child lacks a well-balanced diet, malnutrition occurs, which is evidenced by disease symptoms and processes. Spiritual malnourishment also occurs when we stop feeding on the Word of God and keeping the fellowship of brethren, and also when we do not pray. When in continuous fellowship, we are fed and encouraged, and we grow from one level to another. We achieve much together, and the enemy cannot easily destroy us when well connected. The Bible warns us against neglecting fellowship:

> Not giving up meeting together, as some are in the habit of doing, but encouraging one another— and all the more as you see the Day approaching. (Hebrews 10:25 NIV)

When we fail to follow Christ our savior, our growth is halted, and we become weak. This allows our flesh to arise and dominate over our spiritual strength, and we eventually die spiritually. This is emphasized in God's Word:

> So then, just as you received Christ Jesus as Lord, continue to live your lives in him, rooted and built up in him, strengthened in the faith as you were taught, and overflowing with thankfulness. (Colossians 2:6–7 NIV)

Fighting Wrong Battles and Using Wrong Weapons

As believers, we must understand that the enemy will only fight us when in the service of God and in fellowship where we can grow. His goal is to isolate you so that you do not grow to fruitfulness. An isolated Christian will fight lone battles, and it is easier to succumb to the enemy. We must put on the full armor of God and also understand that our weapons are not carnal. The Bible clearly defines our weapons: "The weapons we fight with are not the weapons of the world. On the contrary, they have divine power to demolish strongholds" (2 Corinthians 10:4 NIV).

We must also remember that our faith in God has helped us to overcome some giants and defeat some spirits, but they can still rise up again if there is no growth. We must defeat every temptation that comes to hinder our growth so as to remain strong and well rooted in God. Keep fighting right; keep believing and stay strong. The battle rages fiercest when victory is around the corner. Understand the battle may cost you. Pay the price of being different as you flourish in your faith. It is the cost of taking the cross.

Wrong Relationships

Association leads to assimilation, which causes impartation. We must watch closely who we are walking with. If our faith does not agree, then we have to separate ourselves and stay on the Lord's path. According to psalms 1:1–3 (NIV),

Blessed is the one who does not walk in step with the wicked or stand in the way that sinners take or sit in the company of mockers, but whose delight is in the law of the Lord, and who meditates on his law day and night. That person is like a tree planted by streams of water, which yields its fruit in season and whose leaf does not wither whatever they do prospers.

We must know our place, the right association, and stay focused. We must be careful with our associations; our good morals must be preserved intentionally. It is imperative to remember that two cannot walk together unless they agree. Seek God to give you the right connections. This is critical for your faith to abound.

Cultural conflict can be a big hindrance and can also derail us from our faith in a world where culture has allowed and accepted so much ungodliness; we must be sober to discern what is right, godly, and acceptable for our growth as believers. What the culture dictates and is against God is not for us. We must rise in prayer and confront such in the spirit and bring change as we continue to grow and bear fruits in the kingdom of God. What looks or sounds like it is right is not for us. We must defeat all ungodliness through prayer and understanding of the Word of God. Growth is distinguishing right from evil. Hebrews 5:14 (NIV), says, "But solid food is for the mature, who by constant use have trained themselves to distinguish good from evil."

Moreover, spiritual thriving is setting an example for believers in speech, conduct, love, faith, and purity. We are the children of the light and the salt of the world. The light in us must illuminate the darkness in the world today, and our influence must impact those around us.

> But set an example for the believers in speech, in conduct, in love, in faith and in purity. (1 Timothy 4:12b NIV)

As Christians, we must realize that we have been given the power to influence and shape the value systems of our society, which should be carried through all generations. We have been called to legislate the will of God on earth.

- Who are your associates?
- Are your relationships building or draining you?

Apathy Spirit

"It is what it is" is a common phrase in our world today. Grandparents, parents, and their children are all speaking about it proudly but ignorantly. Just because it happened to your grandfather, it does not have to be your song. I believe God can change and direct everyone's path for the better. Apathy spirit is a dream killer and hijacker of destinies. We must arise in our discernment and denounce it; we must be set free completely from this spirit that suppresses our passion to pursue what God made us be. This enemy to our destiny kills the motivation to fight or serve and puts one in a retreating posture. You must always be in your warrior posture. The enemy can use apathy as a defense mechanism, which then mutes your happiness, leading to depression of every effort, lack of sense of purpose, worth, and meaning in life, hence spiritual, emotional, and even physical death due to hopelessness. We must keep fighting and break through every limitation in our lives. We must be desperate to succeed and go to extreme lengths and depths to achieve it. Through prayer and faith in God, we can break all generational and cultural limitations, in Jesus's name. Prayer is power and can sustain the ability to go beyond our present environment.

- Have you identified areas that need the right nutrition in your life?
- What do you need to do about it?
- Is association delaying your growth? You have the power to prune your relationships!
- What are you fighting with? Identify, fight, overcome, and grow in Jesus's name.

Prayer for Spiritual Growth

> But thanks be to God, who always leads us as captives in Christ's triumphal procession and uses us to spread the aroma of the knowledge of him everywhere. (2 Corinthians 2:14 NIV)

Heavenly Father, I surrender all to You and yield my spirit to You. I want to triumph in my faith and need Your strength. I know in You I am strong. Help and guide me daily to do the right things that will allow excellent growth in my spiritual walk. I declare I will be on purpose and not passive. I refuse to be distracted. I commit to feeding my spirit rightfully by adding the power of prayer and Your Word daily. I will remain rightly connected as I keep my trust in You, Lord. Grant me wisdom and revelation in the knowledge of You. Additionally, enlighten my spiritual sight and understanding as I continue to submit to You daily, Lord. By Your grace, I will overcome every hindrance to my growth. I will prosper and become fruitful in Your kingdom as I continue to humbly seek and serve You. I commit my ways to You so that You can lead me in Your path, in Jesus's name.

CHAPTER 3
How to Prevent Spiritual Failure to Thrive

Just like in the physical, our spiritual growth is important, and every effort must be made to see it happen. When a baby is born, the mother ensures that the baby gets the right food and enough sleep and has health checkups by the doctor to ensure physical, emotional, and psychological well-being. For us to prevent spiritual failure to thrive and stagnation spirit, there are disciplines that demand our commitment and time. God has made each one of us uniquely and has called us for different purposes, but growth is paramount. He does not want us just to survive but to live purposefully and realize our full potential. Through this, we shall be able to make the difference in the world around us and glorify God.

> Blessed is the one who does not walk in step with
> the wicked or stand in the way that sinners take or

sit in the company of mockers, but whose delight is in the law of the Lord, and who meditates on his law day and night. That person is like a tree planted by streams of water, which yields its fruit in season and whose leaf does not wither whatever they do prospers. (Psalm 1:1–3 NIV)

Right Counsel

Godly counsel will enhance our growth in the Lord. The Holy Spirit who lives in us is our helper and guides us. He is our counselor or advocate, and His teaching is the best for our growth. John 14:26 (NIV) says, "But the Advocate, the Holy Spirit, whom the Father will send in my name, will teach you all things and will remind you of everything I have said to you."

Prune your relationships because bad morals corrupt good character. We must pay every cost to sit in the counsel and fellowship of the godly, those of right attitude and faith like us. Such will support you in your growth and progress. Also, submit under your church authority for accountability. As you grow in your faith, depend on God and acknowledge Him as well as yielding to His prompting always, without procrastination of His counsel or instructions.

Do not be misled. "Bad company corrupts good character" (1 Corinthians 15:33 NIV).

The Word of God

The Word of God should be our daily food. Meditating upon it day and night leads to understanding, which yields prosperity and success.

> Keep this Book of the Law always on your lips; meditate on it day and night, so that you may be careful to do everything written in it. Then you will be prosperous and successful. (Joshua 1:8 NIV)

Additionally, the Bible emphasizes the need to feed on the Word of God because man cannot live on bread alone. This means that for us to thrive in our lives, we need not only the physical food (bread) but the spiritual food too (Word of God). Prayer is also part of daily food (drink), which is essential to our growth and success.

> Jesus answered, it is written Man shall not live on bread alone, but on every word that comes from the mouth of God. (Mathew 4:4 NIV)

The Word of God will teach you that nothing is impossible with Him. Study, meditate, pray, and practice His Word. You will grow and become what you were made for. Moreover, the Word of God is our guide, and through it we are able to understand and pursue God's will in our lives. We cannot thrive outside God's will for us. May His Word illuminate your path to great victories.

Your word is a lamp for my feet, a light on my path. (Psalm 119:105 NIV)

The Environment

A farmer is very careful about preparing the garden for a new season. He/she understands if the garden is not ready, it will affect the growth of the new seeds and plants. Your environment is your growth garden. Watch what is in it. Will it enhance your growth and bring transformation or destroy all your efforts, leading to stagnation? We must be well positioned in an environment that is conducive to growth and fruitfulness. It is imperative to associate with people who are positive and on the same path of growth to enhance our advancement and maturity. We should say no to every environment that will lead to sin. A tree requires healthy components and specific atmospheric conditions to thrive. For our spirit man and soul to thrive, we must feed on the right sources and submit to godly growth and discipline. When well positioned, we shall enjoy the flow of the water and nutrients, like a tree planted by the waters that never ceases to produce fruits.

The Lord is our true vine, and we are the branches; we should remain well connected. The gardener's pruning process ensures quality fruits.

Am the true vine, and my father is the gardener. He cuts off every branch in me that bears no fruit, while every branch that does bear fruit, he prunes so that it will be even more fruitful. (John 15:1–2 NIV)

Prayer

Prayer is our powerful weapon. Through prayer, we invite God to our situations. We must keep growing in our prayer life daily. It takes practice to grow. The disciples watched Jesus praying and eventually learned how to do it and apply it. You must intentionally set a time and place of prayer. That is your place of power, and prayer is a tool to receive hidden knowledge and treasures. Attend fellowship and prayer meetings and keep practicing daily. A weak Christian cannot overcome, but when we add prayer to our lives, we become warriors. Moreover, prayer will release power and blessings from God as well as a breakthrough in your affairs. God's power will burst all the confinements and go before you. "The prayer of a righteous person is powerful and effective" (James 5:16b NIV).

When we grow and advance to maturity, then God is glorified as He uses us as noble vessels to demonstrate His acts and manifestations of His power. In the days of Daniel, he purposed to stand up for God, and God used him to show His power.

May this be your desire. There is a lot in store for you, and it is my prayer that as you continue to read this book, everything will get clearer, and you will grow to do exploits in God's kingdom.

- What has helped you in your growth path? Share examples.
- How does the environment affect one's growth?
- What are you struggling with?

CHAPTER 4
Arise and Pursue What You Were Made For

Potential is simply having or showing the capacity to become or develop into something in the future. It can also be defined as an unrealized ability to fulfill a purpose. We were all created for a purpose that produces the potential in us. We all have the potential to reach our destiny and also thrive in the walk of fruitfulness and exploits in the kingdom of God. The process requires commitment, work, and discipline.

And have you completely forgotten this word of encouragement that addresses you as a father addresses his son? It says, my son, do not make light of the Lord's discipline and do not lose heart when he rebukes you because the Lord disciplines the one he loves, and he chastens everyone he accepts as his son. (Hebrews 12:5–6 NIV)

You are on your way to achieve a great level of attainment in your Christian walk. Apply your godly strategies well and keep the discipline. Results are coming. Persistence and diligence are keys to your victory path. Keep praying, trusting, and feeding right spiritually as you let the Holy Spirit guide you. Refuse to be distracted. The instructions (Word of God) can establish you. There is no kingdom without discipline; it is a requirement for us to thrive in both physical and spiritual realms.

As a mother of two athletic girls, I'm a witness that victory on the field of competition depends on teamwork, competence, and excellence. I have seen the coaches encouraging the girls and pushing them hard to reach their full potential and be successful. The girls do not like it all the time, but they must adhere to the instructions and teamwork to make their dream work. This has yielded great victories in their soccer games.

The discipline from physical and spiritual parents and coaches in our lives propels us to victory if we regard it highly and are willing to follow it and persevere through it. On the contrary, if we do not embrace the instructions, weariness and failure find room on our paths, and thriving, which we were made to excel in, becomes unreachable. We must all remember that we have been called to greatness, and we must fight for it. Your destiny is sure in the hands of God, but you must embrace the process of seeing it come to fulfillment. On our success path, we must learn to develop and build the good habits that we admire in those who have been there before us, including our mentors and coaches. This will lead to victory and fulfillment.

In our Christian growth, our Father sees us as sons and daughters with great potential to do exploits for Him and become what we were designed for. He has already set our destiny and expects us to put in work and discipline to reach there. Myles Monroe said, "One of the greatest tragedies in life is to watch potential die untapped!"

I must remind you that you are loaded for your purpose. Find it and pursue it.

In Genesis 37, we read about Joseph and his brothers. He had dreams concerning his destiny, and although he faced great opposition even from his brothers, he did not stop. He lived purposefully to become what he had seen in the dream.

- Do you have a dream?
- What have you seen?
- What have you heard?
- You can live a passionate and purposeful life and become what you dreamt.

Listen to me. Where you are today is a temporary position. It may be in your career, ministry, or family. You are on your way to a great destiny. Stop living by your eyes. Have faith in God and run after your dream. You are loaded for it. Joseph saw it. Your life is not as short as your paycheck or the next bill. There is untapped wealth in you. Unleash that talent and see what God can do through you. The world needs you to plant trees so that the generations can rest in the shade.

Joseph had a dream, and when he told it to his brothers, they hated him even more. He said to them, "Listen to this dream I had: We were binding sheaves of grain out in the field when suddenly my sheaf rose and stood upright, while your sheaves gathered around mine and bowed down to it." His brothers said to him, "Do you intend to reign over us? Will you actually rule us?" And they hated him all the more because of his dream and what he had said. Then he had another dream, and he told it to his brothers. "Listen," he said, "I had another dream, and this time the sun and moon and eleven stars were bowing down to me." When he told his father as well as his brothers, his father rebuked him and said, "What is this dream you had? Will your mother and I and your brothers actually come and bow down to the ground before you?" His brothers were jealous of him, but his father kept the matter in mind. (Genesis 37:5–10 NIV)

Joseph kept on dreaming, despite the opposition. Arise and dream again. There is no law against dreaming. You will achieve it, in Jesus's name.

The Youths

The Lord sees young people as instruments of worship and service to Him. Ecclesiastes 12:1 (NIV) says, "Remember your Creator in the days of your youth, before the day of trouble comes and the years approach when you will say, 'I find no pleasure in them.'" The Lord has equipped the youths with great physical, emotional, and technological strength, and His desire is for you to direct it in His service when you are still young and strong. You were made to make a difference in the church, community, and nations as you serve God in your youth. Focus on God and regard His disciplines as you continue to love Him, pray, and meditate on the Word of God. Furthermore, the fellowship of the brethren keeps you strong and makes it easy for you to thrive to your full potential in the service of God. In Proverbs 8:17–18 (NIV), God promised us His love, honor, and enduring prosperity as we continue to serve Him. Every youth desires to be recognized for their strength and achievements. When we give ourselves fully to God's service, honor is a reward from God. Keep serving and walking in holiness before God. He is faithful and can be trusted to fulfill His promises. "I love those who love me, and those who seek me find me. With me are riches and honor, enduring wealth and prosperity."

I must say that the spiritual affects the physical. When we learn and flourish in our walk with God and service to Him as young people, God honors our efforts, and our physical life is changed too. It becomes easy for us to follow the required disciple in our studies and careers, and we become successful. I have seen this in my life and can confidently testify that where I am today as a pastor's wife, minister, mother, and a seasoned registered nurse was mothered through my dedication to God since my early teenage years. I intentionally spent a lot of time in the church, fellowship, and serving God diligently. I remember one day one of the pastors in the church called me after the morning glory service and asked me what I wanted in the house of God since I was always there. I was not looking for anything else but wanted to be spiritually fed and just have encounters with the Lord. Our father is a just God; He will not forget your works and dedication. He honors those who love Him. Diligently be available, be consistent, learn more, be teachable, find a mentor, and intentionally stay in touch with family, trustworthy friends, and your church family.

As youths, there are many challenges and enemies of our faith, but if we follow the right counsel and regard the discipline as above, we will succeed. You don't have to be like everyone else; you can say no to every unrighteousness and ungodliness even in this century. Peer pressure should not derail or push you to give in to the desires of the sinful nature; it is the devil's strategy to commandeer your destiny. Fight like a winner who knows that there is a reward after the race. "Do you not know that in a race all the runners run, but only one gets the prize? Run in such a way as to get the prize" (1 Corinthians 9:24 NIV).

Become God's mouthpiece that He can use to minister godliness, holiness, and righteousness to the young generation at such a time like this. Seeing your destiny fulfilled is your greatest reward. Honor God with your body and stay pure as you serve Him. Let His Word be your light and flee from every sin that comes to distract or defile you from your path of faith. "How can a young person stay on the path of purity? By living according to your word" (Psalm 119:9 NIV).

Submit fully to your parents, church, and community authority and be accountable. You will succeed. You do not have to be like anyone else around you. You are a difference maker. Say no to peer pressure and stand up for your God. Your generation and future generations need your strength. Hold onto your integrity like Joseph in the Bible. He was a young man who overcame the temptation of sexual sin. You can overcome every temptation by God's grace and wisdom. Run every race with a focus. You will win, in Jesus's name.

In Acts 2:17 (NIV), the Bible talks about sons and daughters prophesying and young men seeing visions. There is a hidden strength in you as a young person. Nations are waiting to hear what the heavens are saying through you. Seek God and feed your gift through His Word, prayer, and commitment to the right teachings. You are loaded with answers for the nations.

"In the last days, God says, I will pour out my Spirit on all people. Your sons and daughters will prophesy, your young men will see visions your old men will dream dreams."

- What do you hope to become?
- What is your vision?
- Who are you following?
- Who are you accountable to?
- The Spirit of the Lord is upon you. Your vision is valid. Pursue!

It is not too early to activate your potential. God is a God of purpose and the source of your potential. Follow the right guidance, write your vision down, connect with God and your trusted resources, and pursue it.

When I was a young girl in middle and high school, I loved to help everyone in my village. I spent time braiding young girls' hair, making them sweaters, and making embroidery tablecloths for women. My mom recognized that and knew I had a gift. She started talking to me about it, and I recall her words almost daily: "Maggy, you love to help. I think you can become a very good nurse." Although I was too young to understand it all then, by God's grace, I conceived those words. I started asking questions about nursing, and the more I learned about it, the more I desired to become one. I must say by God's grace, prayer, obedience, and hard work, I became what my mother had helped me visualize. As I mentioned in the dedication, I am living a life of resilience, fulfillment, and fruitfulness because I pursued my purpose by God's grace, not only in nursing but also ministry. The Lord Has given me the grace to serve Him and humanity, and I enjoy doing it in and out of season. I believe God has preserved me this far because of the vision. Do not be derailed. Do not lose hope. That which looks impossible can be possible if you put your faith in God and activate that dormant ability in you. God is faithful. He will preserve you too.

I trust that as you continue reading this book, you will be strengthened and encouraged, and your inner eyes will be unveiled to see what God has in store for you. Keep pushing. You will become.

I love this powerful quote by Warren Buffet, one of the world's most successful men:

> Surround yourself with people who push you to do and be better. No drama or negativity, just higher goals and higher motivation. good times and positive energy; No jealousy or hate. Simply bringing out the absolute best in each other.

Please choose well, prune your relationships, and create time for growth and success in every aspect of your life. Purpose to become better daily, and do not just like your talent, calling, or career; live it passionately and purposefully.

Men and Women

We have all been called to thrive and do exploits both in our walks of faith and physical lives. Exploits are noble achievements, but we cannot achieve them if there is no growth in our daily walk. We must allow the right connections in our lives, have the right attitude, remain positive, overcome fear, and embrace coaching and discipline so that we can grow to fruitfulness. Being fully grafted into Jesus Christ leads to the strength that leads to victory and success. Even when we meet rocky paths on our way to full potential, our faith continues to grow and keeps us going.

Every relationship starts with just meeting the person, and then the connection grows as both parties continue to fellowship and work toward the blossoming of their relationship. If one party blunders, it weakens the relationship, which eventually succumbs due to halted growth. Knowing God deeply demands a lot of sacrifice and effectiveness in our time management to be able to maintain growth in the relationship. We must intentionally be willing and committed to creating time to be in the Lord's presence, which means it is critical to invest in our relationship with God, to know Him just like in a physical relationship where friends spend time together to become well acquainted. We must study His Word and seek Him in prayer until we get to understand Him, His ways, and His works. The Bible emphasizes the importance of drawing closer to God and staying connected with Him.

> Submit yourselves, then, to God. Resist the devil,
> and he will flee from you. Come near to God and
> he will come near to you. (James 4:7–8 NIV)

Keep drawing closer to your God. He will draw closer to you, and your relationship will blossom.

Moses had intimacy with God; he knew Him personally, as well as His ways. I confidently believe Moses applied personal initiative and responsibility in his walk of faith to reach this level. His selflessness and asceticism yielded victory in knowing God and understanding Him. The Bible records that God spoke to Moses face-to-face. "The Lord would speak to Moses face to face, as one speaks to a friend" (Exodus 33:11 NIV).

This means Moses had grown to his full potential, where God could share His heart with him face-to-face. In an intimate relationship, we become one with the person, just like in marriage;

a husband and wife know each other and understand each other's ways. Knowing someone to this extent means we not only know about their reputation, but we are also connected at a higher level than others. Such a relationship yields benefits for both parties. It is a productive and fulfilling relationship. Moses sacrificed and even left his family behind to know, understand, and follow God. He understood his role in the relationship and did not want anything to stand as a hindrance.

On our path to full potential, we must understand that self-sacrifice is an expectation; sometimes we have to separate ourselves from others to cultivate our relationship with God and find Him. When we find God, then we find ourselves, and we can confidently share the benefits of our growth with others, even in the physical, which is fruitful. Moses spent time on the mountain seeking God's counsel, and this strengthened his relationship with God. The enemy will try to use distraction to hinder you from reaching your full potential, but remain focused and rise in prayer to fortify your discernment. Allow the Holy Spirit of God to lead you as you make the right choices and stay connected with your Father.

The right connection ensures growth and stability, and fruitfulness will be the result. No one can do exploits unless he/she knows God. We must trust God for an irresistible impulse to get understanding and knowledge of who He is, His operations, and promises for us. Reading and meditating upon His Word, prayer, fasting, and fellowship will open us to a higher mastery level. If this lacks, then we remain in status quo, weariness sets in, and failure to thrive might be our next diagnosis. This means we cannot enjoy the benefits of the relationship with God. It is His promise for us. In Proverbs 8:17–19 (NIV), God promises us His love, honor and riches: "I love those who love me, and those who seek me find me. With me are riches and honor enduring wealth and prosperity. My fruit is better than fine gold; what I yield surpasses choice silver." These are great promises for the children of God, but the enemy is out to hinder them. Let us be sober, keep watch as we pray, and defeat him in Jesus's name.

Full potential in our calling, career, family, and ministry is our goal, and we must triumph in the battle against the devil, cultural conflict, and our mindset to reach there. Where you are in any of the above is your temporary position. Do not stop there. There is untapped power in you. Your destiny awaits. You can do all things through Christ who strengthens you.

It is at this level that we can make a difference in the church and society. We are strong to legislate God's will in the world around us. The Lord is looking for problem solvers, wise counselors who can advise those in authority, leaders who will govern His people in wisdom, and strong men and women who will prayerfully confront cultural and gender conflict that is against the Word of God. Therefore, if there is no growth in our lives and we fail, then we continue being part of the problem in the society instead of being the answer that the Lord expects us to be.

Our society does not need any more patients with failure to thrive but is looking for men and women who are well equipped spiritually, emotionally, psychologically, financially, and physically to lead and offer answers as the light and the salt to the children, youth, men, and women who have lost hope and are vulnerable to attacks and arrows of the enemy. The Bible says we are the salt of the earth. Let's take our position and influence the world around us to be a better place. We are strong. We carry the right flavor for our society. Let's season it. Light and salt belong to the world that we live in. Let our influence be felt up to the uttermost. Colossians 1:13 (NIV) says, "For He Has rescued us from the dominion of darkness; And brought us into the Kingdom of the Son He loves." This helps us to understand more about the light of God. It is not just the absence of darkness but also the overcoming presence of God that breaks yokes, liberates, and transforms. When we walk in it and ignite others in our sphere of influence, we shall see God's power manifested in our success path, families, church, and the nations.

- Have you thought of successful parenting as prosperity and fruitfulness?

As parents, we should understand that parenting is a kingdom mandate. Successful parenting is victory for generations, church, and society. God sees as us His representatives in the kingdom that we belong to. As His ambassadors, He has entrusted us with generations. We must teach them genuine faith, instruct them on how to safely fly in this world that is changing daily, and equip them for their destinies and godly purposes. Our parenting must carry power to nurture, instruct, and command change in Jesus's name. We must follow the kingdom strategies and not the cultural systems that have allowed and accepted everything as right. Our children must be taught to successfully confront such and bring change. We must role model in our parenting. Our homes are the primary units for teaching right morals, genuine faith, boundaries, and consistency to our children. Additionally, we must teach them how to pay attention to godly wisdom and how to apply the knowledge, faith, and wisdom in life. Genuine faith gives hope and empowers! Our world needs well-equipped warriors who can fix the broken systems. Fathers must arise and instruct their children daily as well as offer sacrifices for them every morning like Job did. Instructors are supposed to role model and are always present. When fathers are absent, children will fail because they will have no one to counsel, correct what is not right, guide, and cancel the wrong that has been spoken against the children. Coaches and instructors give live demonstrations on how to play or perform. The players are then expected to give return demonstration as evidence of competency. Fathers, you can not instruct remotely or through your acquaintances daily and expect the children to be successful. You will fail in your success path as a parent, and the generations will fail. Your kingdom assignment as a father demands your presence! Arise to the plate and embrace your role. Generations are waiting. Children who have not been taught to honor physical authority will have problems honoring spiritual authority.

"Listen, my son, to your father's instruction and do not forsake your mother's teaching" (Proverbs 1:8 NIV).

Fathers, be careful where your footsteps are leading your children; their success depends on you.

Mothers must arise and teach godliness and faith and pray for their children. When mothers fail to pray, no one else is travailing for the children. Mothers have more power at hand than the king's scepter. We have the kingdom authority. Seize every moment and teach, mentor, nurture, and support. In the Bible, Timothy was well equipped in faith that he had learned from his grandmother and mother. Paul, an apostle, was able to trust him as a coworker in the ministry because he had learned genuine faith.

> I am reminded of your sincere faith, which first lived in your grandmother Lois and in your mother Eunice and, I am persuaded, now lives in you also. (2 Timothy 1:5 NIV)

When the children are well equipped and empowered, they will be successful in not only careers but also in behavior, character, speech, and every aspect of their lives. They will be hope carriers and will also teach others, just as Timothy taught the congregations right beliefs, proper conduct, and respect. We have the opportunity to amplify their small voices to be voices of hope, joy, love, godliness, righteousness, and healing in a world that desperately needs it. Let us empower and secure their destiny in God through right parenting.

> These commandments that I give you today are to be on your hearts. Impress them on your children. Talk about them when you sit at home and when you walk along the road, when you lie down and when you get up. Tie them as symbols on your hands and bind them on your foreheads. Write them on the doorframes of your houses and on your gates. (Deuteronomy 6:4–9 NIV)

In a world full of challenges and distractions, it is very easy to miss the opportunities and avenues that God has given us as parents to fulfil the parenting mandate. Let's be careful what our children hear, see, and do at home as they walk, sleep, and even as they rise up. We must diligently, rightly influence in wisdom and teach godly ordinances that lead to victory. God's Word will give them good success. What we do in our family determines the level of success for our generations, church, and society!

The schools and society at large are waiting for us to send children who have been taught and instructed at home so that they can be difference makers. It is against the kingdom discipline and principles to expect the schools to teach and instruct our children for us. This is why the world is so broken. Morals are corrupted because parents have failed to mentor, nurture, teach, instruct, and support. It is time to empower our children and our future generations. Parents can no longer depend on yesterday's wisdom and victories. The world is changing daily, and we must be sober and seek godly ideas and strategies in our parenting. Pray and commit to remain active, available, resourceful, and influential in your parenting assignment.

In our church, the women's ministry is called Women of Strength. After seeking God, it was very clear that as women living in today's era, we must be clothed with spiritual, emotional, psychological, and physical strength to bear, nurture, coach, mentor, and role model that which we want to see in our families, church, and society. We are supposed to be the women who give the right counsel to all around us and also watch over the households that the Lord has entrusted to us. Deborah in the Bible is a good example of a woman who understood her position and spent time in the presence of the Lord. The Bible records she gave the right counsel as a prophet and a judge in Israel.

> Now Deborah, a prophet, the wife of Lappidoth, was leading Israel at that time. She held court under the Palm of Deborah between Ramah and Bethel in the hill country of Ephraim, and the Israelites went up to her to have their disputes decided. (Judges 4:4–5 NIV)

Hannah was another strong pillar of God's grace and humility. She surrendered totally to God and received the blessing of a son through persistence in prayer. She overcame the enemies that surrounded her path at a crucial time of her life, and she became the mother to a prophet that Israel needed. We must align ourselves with the heavenly plans for us so as to make the difference we were made for. Let's pursue to understand our seasons, be well positioned, and make God the center of it. This will keep us strong, and we shall for sure fulfil what God Has called us for.

The enemies of your destiny will be there to distract, disarm, and ensure you are not well connected with the source of your strength, but keep moving. Both Deborah and Hannah persisted in the Lord's presence, and they fulfilled their purposes. The secret is staying in tune with God and in His perfect will.

When we are strong, then we are well positioned to make the right decisions for our families, church, and society. We shall also be able to fight for one another in love and stand in the gap as difference makers in the world that so badly needs it. The key is being open to godly discipline that pushes us to our full potential. Spending time in prayer, reading, meditating upon the Word of God, being in fellowship, and connecting with our destiny helpers are all critical. When we spend time with God, He washes, counsels, and prunes us. These encounters equip us for our destiny and influence others.

Myles Monroe said, "People generally fall into one of three groups: the few who make things happen, the many who watch things happen, and the overwhelming majorities who have no notion of what happens. Every person is either a creator of fact or a creature of circumstance. He either puts color into his environment or like a chameleon, takes color from his environment."

Let us spring up and fight to make this world a better place. We can make the right things happen in our families, church, and society and put color in our environment instead of taking the color away like the chameleon.

There is creativity, riches, hope, power, and reserved energy in you. Put it into action.

- Where are you in your life?
- What do you want to see happen in families, church, and society?
- Are you battling with a stagnation spirit?
- Is your mindset your hurdle?

- What are you doing to add color to the environment?
- Do not perish for lack of vision or wisdom. Learn and put the knowledge into action!

Arise and take your position. You can vanquish every limitation. Your destiny is sure and safe in God. Keep going, keep believing, keep learning, keep working, and keep growing.

Please Declare This with Me!

> What you decide on will be done, and light will
> shine on your ways. (Job 22:28 NIV)

Lord, I thank You for preserving me this far. I declare that I have a great purpose and I am loaded for it. There is untapped wealth, strength, success, and ability in me for me, my family, society, and the nations. I will not stop because You are with me. I am not too young or too old to pursue Your purpose for me. I will be the light and salt and make the right things happen around me. I will not take color away from my environment anymore but will be the person that You created me to be. I will be called upon to counsel others and create facts and faith in the world. I will walk in Your divine wisdom, knowledge, and understanding and overcome every hurdle on my path and bring glory to Your name. The nations, church, families, and generations will benefit from me, my thoughts, my works, and my success, in Jesus's name.

CHAPTER 5
Hurdles to Reaching Your Full Potential

Fear

To understand the effects of fear on our full potential, we must first learn what fear is. It is very important to note that fear is a torment that hinders progress. It is believing that something bad is going to happen. It leads to emotional, psychological, and even physical distress. Additionally, fear hinders success. When people fear losing everything or failing, they fail to take the right steps to advance or even take risks that would impel them to a higher level. Some even cease trying at all, limiting their opportunities to reach their full potential. Fear causes most of us to buckle and settle for less than God's best for us.

> But now, this is what the Lord says he who created you, Jacob, he who formed you, Israel: Do not

fear, for I have redeemed you; I have summoned
you by name; you are mine. (Isaiah 43:1 NIV)

The Lord commands us not to fear or worry and the phrase "fear
not" is used at least eighty times in the Bible. This should be our
encouragement, and as we focus and wait on God, we should not
allow the enemy to use fear to destroy our hope and limit our
victories. Hold onto your loving and caring Father who loves and
calls you by name. Arise and take your position. You have not
been given the spirit of fear but of power and love and a sound
mind.

For the Spirit God gave us does not make us
timid, but gives us power, love and self-discipline.
(2 Timothy 1:7 NIV)

Fear can cripple you. In Numbers 13:33, the Israelites believed
in their minds that they were like grasshoppers before giants.
This empowered the giants, who themselves had been afraid of
the children of Israel. Fear caused the Israelites not to fulfill the
call of God.

We saw the Nephilim there (the descendants of
Anak come from the Nephilim). We seemed like
grasshoppers in our own eyes, and we looked the
same to them. (Numbers 13:33 NIV)

Arise and confront every new opportunity and challenge and walk
through open doors. Do not walk in fear; allow the Lord to guide

you into His perfect will for you. You were made to thrive, so keep moving. See things from the Lord's perspective. You will win.

- How has fear affected your abounding path?
- How are you going to overcome it?

The Past

The experiences that we have gone through should not determine or define us or our destiny. How we handle and act in our present moments will determine our tomorrow. Staying focused on the present and working toward our goals will keep us away from dwelling on the past. You will be tempted by the enemy to dwell on your past, but stay alert; do not allow him to drain your energy. Keep moving on. Focus on the new things that the Lord is doing. Fuel yourself up through the word of God, fellowship, and devotion to prayer. Allow God to order your steps as you work on your faith path, career, and personal life.

> Forget the former things; do not dwell on the past. See, I am doing a new thing! Now it springs up; do you not perceive it? I am making a way in the wilderness and streams in the wasteland. (Isaiah 43:18–19 NIV)

Do not let the past rule you; it will rob you of the opportunities to reach your full potential.

Your past does not define who you are. Additionally, do not allow the family history to determine how far you can go. Do not be a slave of the past. You may have been hurt, wounded, or bruised before, but there is hope for you. Job 14:7 (NIV) says, "At least there is hope for a tree: If it is cut down, it will sprout again, and its new shoots will not fail."

You have not been uprooted. Invigorate your roots again by the Word of God, prayer, and fellowship. Study more and get more qualified. An old root can still produce new fruit. See your scars as a sign of strength, victory, and healing, but do not allow them to hold you hostage. Forgive and let go of the old hurts and allow God to heal you. Open your heart for God and the new things that He is doing and close it to things that can hurt you again or drag you back to the past. Develop a strong capacity to deal with offenses. Holding onto the past is one of the habits that drain your energy and strength. Fight hard and purposefully. Live out the full potential of your calling, career, and family.

- Is your past holding you captive?
- Is it time to recharge your faith batteries?
- Remain focused. It is your springtime!

Mindset

Mindset is your established set of attitudes, which can be positive or negative. A positive mindset is attractive and is everything; for there to be a change in our lives, our mindset must be renewed. We must remain consistent and set our mind on the positive things that lead to success and maintaining it. Who we are and our actions are a total product of our thoughts and meditation. Additionally, no one can rise above the level of their mindset.

> Do not conform to the pattern of this world, but be transformed by the renewing of your mind. Then you will be able to test and approve what God's will is—his good, pleasing and perfect will. (Romans 12:2 NIV)

The will of God is His idea concerning you or something in your life; it is His desire for you. This means that mind renewal should be a continuous process and will allow you to understand what God has in store for you and fight for it. Moreover, through mind renewal, we can look at circumstances differently; instead of seeing how overwhelming they are, we begin to focus on the great God who is not limited. David refused to focus on Goliath's strength and spoke about His able God who he trusted in. God gave him victory.

Your mindset is powerful and can change values and systems, but be careful; it can limit your prayers, despite praying well, and also limit God. We must embrace our vision in our minds and push to achieve it. A small mindset cannot achieve what God has called you to do. Have a growth mindset. A grasshopper mindset is a tragedy to your vision.

You were made to thrive. Believe in your dream and work toward it. Always remember you can never rise above the level of your thoughts.

You must always remember that you are a product of your thoughts, and it is paramount that you become the master of your thoughts. Sift your thought life and filter out anything that would hinder your potential. Your thoughts are powerful. Surrender them to God, who is the ultimate source, and use them to create, innovate, strategize, and succeed through God's guidance.

Examining your thoughts is important. According to 1 Peter 1:13, we are supposed to gird up the loins of our mind. Examine what your thoughts are chasing after and what your words are gathering to you. Always remember that the world within not only colors the world without, but it is also its blueprint. Think progress, confess it, speak life to your dreams, and achieve it in Jesus's name.

> When you pursue knowledge, wisdom, and truth, your mouth will speak words out of that abundance that will frame your world. (Cindy Trimm)

- How can you take control of your thoughts?

Lack of Vision

Vision is a function of the heart; it is the ability to think progressively and to see future possibilities. You must enlarge your visual capacity by getting closer to God. The closer we are to God, the clearer the vision and the better the perspective. Pray and seek God to open your eyes to see your abilities in a new light. You must see yourself doing, gaining, and becoming more in Jesus's name. Where there is no vision, people perish. Pray bigger, expect bigger, and trust God to take you to that place you have never been and must get to. Persist until you reach your full potential. God had to deal with Abraham's vision. He wanted to enlarge him, but He knew Abraham's vision needed a change.

> The Lord said to Abram after Lot had parted from him, "Look around from where you are, to the north and south, to the east and west. All the land that you see I will give to you and your offspring forever. I will make your offspring like the dust of the earth, so that if anyone could count the dust, then your offspring could be counted. Go, walk through the length and breadth of the land, for I am giving it to you." (Genesis 13:14–17 NIV)

The only limitation was his vision. You must break through this barrier and have the vision to succeed. Remember, potential is not what you have done; it is what you have not done or become. The east, west, south, and north are waiting for you to enlarge your boundaries.

Pray to God to give you the grace of favor to connect with relevant and anointed people and resources to propel you to your destiny. See yourself there already. Take every step and risk to get there like the woman with the issue of the blood in Matthew 9:20–22 (NIV):

> Just then a woman who had been subject to bleeding for twelve years came up behind him and

49

touched the edge of his cloak. She said to herself, "If I only touch his cloak, I will be healed." Jesus turned and saw her. "Take heart, daughter," he said, "your faith has healed you." And the woman was healed at that moment.

Risk of faith and courage will lead you to victory. She had already visualized herself healed. Unless you see it, you are not entitled to it!

- What can you see?
- How far can you see?
- What you see today determines what you will possess or become.
- How far are you willing to risk?

Helen Keller said, "The greatest tragedy in life is people who have no vision." Refuse to be the tragedy or even part of it. Run with what you envision. Remember you will never possess beyond your vision.

Lack of Capacity

Capacity is the ability to receive, hold, or contain. I can simply call it the ability to grow. Every individual was created with great capacity in them, but it is the responsibility of each person to tap into it. What does that mean? You see, the source of everything is in the spirit. We are spiritual beings with a soul but living in a body. On your growth path, you will face adversity, and your strength must be enough to handle any hurdles along the way. You must remain resilient and stay connected to God and your support system. It takes time, strength, and support from your trusted helpers to reach your full potential. Keep pushing. Do not faint.

Proverbs 24:10 says, "If you faint in the day of adversity, your strength is small." This means you must seek the things that keep your capacity high. You are an overcomer. Let me remind you that overcomers do not quit; they fight tirelessly through adversity to their victory. I have seen God's victory in situations that have been very challenging through consistent prayer and believing that in times of adversity, we can still win victories. We must embrace the Word of God, prayer, fasting, and fellowship even in battles. This is your diet for strength in adversity.

The Lord told Jeremiah that before he was formed in his mother's womb, God knew him. He also spoke about his potential capacity of being a prophet to the nations. Although God spoke about Jeremiah being a prophet to the nations, it was his duty to tap into it and grow in it. "Before I formed you in the womb, I knew you before you were born, I set you apart, I appointed you as a prophet to the nations" (Jeremiah 1:5 NIV).

Additionally, the Bible says that we were all created in the image and likeness of God. That means we have a godly capacity like our Father. Jesus explained to the disciples their capacity before He ascended to heaven. "Very truly I tell you, whoever believes in me will do the works I have been doing, and they will do even greater things than these, because I am going to the father" (John 14:12 NIV).

Lack of capacity in us will limit God's power in our lives. There are many victories for us to win, so let's stay focused.

❖ How to Tap into Our God-Given Capacity

- **Salvation**
  We must be born again according to God's Word. Salvation is the key for us to see the kingdom of God and His blessings. Children inherit the attributes of their parents. We must believe and trust in God; without faith, we cannot please God. Jesus replied, "Very truly I tell you, no one can see the kingdom of God unless they are born again" (John 3:3 NIV).

  Spiritual strength is how built you are on the inside. It activates your spirit and connection to the divine from within, giving you the power you need to live a life of purpose and fulfillment. Moreover, spiritual capacity is the degree to which you understand yourself and what you want most, the foundation of a fulfilling life, and you must build it. If you do not know what you want or what your purpose is, you might spend all your energy running in the wrong direction. This leads to burnout, frustration, and unfulfillment. Everyone must develop spiritual, intellectual, physical, and emotional capacity.

- **Divine Power**
  Divine power will propel us to tapping into our capacity. According to the Bible, we shall receive power when the

Holy Spirit comes upon us. So, the Holy Spirit's power in us will guide and help us in fulfilling our assignment.

> But you will receive power when the Holy Spirit comes on you; and you will be my witnesses in Jerusalem, and in all Judea and Samaria, and to the ends of the earth. (Acts 1:8 NIV)

- **Pursuing God's Will**

  We must pursue God's will in our lives because our full capacity is in His will for our lives. Just like we mentioned Jeremiah's purpose above, God has a purpose for each one of us. We must seek to know God's will and pursue it.

- **Take Responsibility**

  Your capacity, strength, and growth are your responsibility, meaning you must intentionally give attention to them. Stir up what God has put in you. Create time to pray. Meditate on God's Word and exercise your abilities. Your prayer capacity is equivalent to your vision. If you want to serve God as a vessel of honor, you must increase your capacity for ministry. Purge yourself and become an honorable vessel that God can use at any level.

  > Those who cleanse themselves from the latter will be instruments for special purposes, made holy, useful to the Master and prepared to do any good work. (2 Timothy 2:21 NIV)

Study the Word of God and spend time in His presence. The more you know Him, the stronger you become. Intimacy with God will increase your capacity for knowledge. You will also learn and understand the enemy's strategies, which will help you understand how to fight him effectively. Keep enlarging your capacity in every aspect, and you will be successful. Do not perish for lack of knowledge.

- How much can you contain?
- What do you need to do to enlarge yourself?

Your Last Success

This might sound odd or new to many, but your former glory can be your biggest hindrance and limitation to your growth and victory in the next level of your life. The victory of yesterday can hinder what God wants you to do presently. He is still doing new things. Stay open to Him, and you will see the new spring forth. Do not let your previous success blind you. Potential is not what you have done but that which you have not or become yet. It is the untapped power in you that the world needs. I will say it again: where you are in life is a temporary position. Keep pushing; there is more. You trusted in God for your current achievement, and He helped you this far. Trust in Him again for another higher glory. Do not allow yesterday's power to destroy your today and tomorrow. Be open to see what He is doing and will do. There is a new song within you. Be watchful. The spirit of complacency can easily creep in, decamp, and seek what the Lord has set before you. Do not be too comfortable in your current position. In the book of Deuteronomy, the Lord spoke to the Israelites through Moses and told them to break camp. It was only then that they could see the land that He had set before them. Possession comes after breaking camp.

> The Lord our God said to us at Horeb, "You have stayed long enough at this mountain. Break camp and advance into the hill country of the Amorites; go to all the neighboring peoples in the Arabah, in the mountains, in the western foothills, in the Negev, and along the coast, to the land of the Canaanites and Lebanon, as far as the great river, the Euphrates. See, I have given you this land. Go in and take possession of the land the Lord swore he would give to your fathers—to Abraham, Isaac, and Jacob—and their descendants after them." (Deuteronomy 1:6–8 NIV)

- Leaving your comfort zone brings abounding. Are you willing to get out of your comfort zone?
- Are you willing to decamp?
- It takes courage and humility to follow God's instructions, what is He saying. Obey and you will succeed.

Moreover, when we live by our eyes, we cannot achieve much. We will be content with yesterday's victory, but God wants us to do more exploits. The more we open ourselves to Him and growth, the higher we shall soar. The Word of God teaches us that our God is abundant in power, and His understanding is beyond measure. We can tap into this power and allow it to work in our lives by trusting in Him, spending time in His presence, and seeking more. Ask for His understanding, which is infinite, and create more. The opportunities may look like they have been saturated, or maybe you feel like you have come to the absolute end of your ability, but trust in His power. You have the power to create something new. Do not settle on your temporary position. It is all possible with our God. Your life is not as short as your paycheck or the next bill. Arise. The Lord is not limited. Do not put Him in your last success box. He is at work in us and able to do exceedingly and abundantly above all that we ask or think according to the power that works in us. May you experience the love of Christ and His unlimited power and ability in your next success level. His love is too great to understand fully, but may you be made complete with the fullness of life and power that comes from God.

> Now to Him who is able to do immeasurably more than all we ask or imagine, according to His power that is at work within us. (Ephesians 3:20 NIV)

Pride

Pride is a short word but can lead to great destruction. This negative attitude can destroy not only an individual but also their destiny. No one is immune to this giant of having unduly high opinions of self from achievements, associations, or external praise. We must all fight and resist the pressure of pride on the path to our destiny. A great victory is coming our way, and we might be tempted to be very conscious of our dignity negatively. At every level that the Lord takes us, we must do humility checks and embrace it as a lifestyle, always remembering God as the Ebenezer.

Moreover, as we continue to prosper and many praises come our way, never let any amount of praise, achievement, or influence lead to pride. Fight and resist it as you keep climbing your ladder of honor in humility. Be on your knees more than on your tongue. The Word of God warns us against pride. It goes before destruction (Proverbs 16:18). This means we must be very cautious with what we feel and what others say about our success. The minute we stop acknowledging God's grace, our downfall starts. Let our attitude and character have the value that can change other people's lives.

> Pride brings a person low, but the lowly in spirit
> gain honor. (Proverbs 29:23 NIV)

If we want to maintain our success story, we must humble ourselves at every level, and we shall honorably rise to exploits.

- Have you heard pride goes before a fall? This is a must fight!
- When was your last humility check? Can you make it a lifestyle?
- Humility demands paying the cost, but you will shine to great heights.

The Enemies Without

You have worked hard to overcome the enemies within you or internal hindrances to your destiny, but I must remind you about the enemies that gather along your path. These are the enemies from the outside environment whose goal is to ensure that you do not accomplish your purpose. Many people will come to discourage, distract, criticize, and judge, and others will be jealous of your success and will come to you, determined to see you compromise or give up.

Stay focused, do not shrink back, and do not give in to the voice of the enemy. He is out to see you get weary and fail on your noble mission.

Additionally, the enemy comes to steal, kill, and destroy your destiny, but the one in you is greater, and you have victory in God. Remember, you must remain well connected to God and the trusted people around you. You will be tempted to doubt God, but do not fall into the devil's trap. Your destiny is sure, and God will see you through. There is a great reward ahead.

Moreover, keep your faith in God, do not compromise, keep praising God, fast, pray, seek fellowship, and study the Word of God. It will keep your faith sturdy and well connected with God. Through His Word, you will learn that no weapon formed against you shall prosper. Hannah overcame the enemies of her destiny through prayer, resilience, and humility. Cultivate these, and you will overcome. Do not let your enemies' words control you. This will open doors for everyone else to control you. Hannah could have failed in her purpose if she allowed Peninnah's or her husband, Elkana's, words to destabilize her faith and vision.

> "No weapon forged against you will prevail, and you will refute every tongue that accuses you. This is the heritage of the servants of the Lord, and this is their vindication from me," declares the Lord. (Isaiah 54:17 NIV)

I pray that your external enemies will provoke you to believe more, pray, seek, serve, and shine brighter even as you develop the fortitude to handle the higher glory coming your way. The promises of God will remain true for you. Stand on them, be relentless, keep pushing, and trust in His peace and grace.

> Let us then approach God's throne of grace with confidence, so that we may receive mercy and find grace to help us in our time of need. (Hebrews 4:16 NIV)

- What is your greatest enemy or limitation? Discuss both the internal and external ones.
- Do you feel like you have reached your absolute end in ability?
- Is your past still limiting you?
- Has fear crippled you?
- Is your capacity limiting you?
- Are you struggling with pride?
- How are you going to overcome it all?

There are many enemies of our destiny, and we must fearlessly do everything possible to defeat them and rise to victory. Keep fighting, keep your eyes and ears open, and keep growing in your capacity. You belong to the resilient tribe that does not give up or get weary. A tribe that focuses on the prize after winning the race despite the distractions. The great tribe that desires to do exploits in the society, church, family, and God's kingdom in and out of season. This is the tribe of kingdom seekers and builders.

There is a higher glory waiting. You are not limited because you trust in a God who is not limited in power and ability. His understanding is infinite. Do not allow the enemy to ensnare and entangle you through fear. Your destiny awaits!

Additionally, do not allow the present or past conditions in your life or the world to discourage or disarm you. Keep praying, act, glorify God by trusting in Him, and He will answer in His power.

You will subdue every hurdle in Jesus's name. Keep running the race. Keep winning victories to your destiny.

Declaration

> No, in all these things we are more than conquerors
> through him who loved us. (Romans 8:37 NIV)

I declare that I will conquer every battle within and without. I will remain focused, resilient, and relentless, focusing on God and His purpose for me. There is sufficient grace and mercy to take me through my success path, and I will not be weary. I will keep my eyes focused on God's victory even as I seek God in perseverance. Every hurdle and mountain on my success path will become a plateau because the lord is with me, and He will open every door ahead of me. The Lord will carry me through to victory as I glorify Him on my path through persistence, sturdy faith, faithfulness, and humility. I will not give up or compromise my faith even as I rise to higher glory in Jesus's name.

CHAPTER 6
It Is Your Time

We have all gone through experiences in life that make us think that there are no more opportunities for us, but every day is a new day loaded with new hope, strength, possibilities, and opportunities. Instead of losing hope, we need to persist and pursue every new and available opportunity available for our growth and fulfillment. The Lord has given us the capability to stretch and be creative in our world. Even when every opportunity seems like it has been saturated, seek God for divine wisdom and creativity to go beyond those borders and create something new.

Today is your dawn of new possibilities. Take charge. Control how your day and season goes. Declare and command your dawn to cooperate with your purpose and destiny. Time is your gift from God. Plan well and use it to intentionally glorify God in all you do. Continue to seek, grow, and serve God and humankind as you pursue greater heights in your life. Remember, it is your responsibility to create time to achieve what you were designed for. You will never have time that you never created! Everyone has twenty-four hours every day; whoever uses it well will continue to grow and flourish.

Past failures should not define you or dictate the way you move from one level to the other. Focusing on the positive will lead you to victory and prevent the cycle of negativity that comes from a negative focus. It is a choice you have to make. Choose to remain positive and focus on your full potential. Refuse to be derailed, deterred, delayed, defeated, or destroyed by the past or current situation. You are victorious. Envision it, speak it, and receive it in Jesus's name. Your past failures may be on people's tongues, but your future is in the hands of God. Trust in Him.

> But I trust in you, Lord; I say, "You are my God."
> My times are in your hands; deliver me from the
> hands of my enemies, from those who pursue me.
> (Psalm 31: 14–15 NIV)

I would like to pray with you if you have been walking in the past and your progress has been deterred by the enemy. God can set you free, and you can set your mind and heart to trust in God as you let go.

Please pray this prayer to break the bondage of your past:

"Heavenly Father, I have undergone a lot, and it has hurt me greatly, but today I want to let go and trust in You. I know I cannot do it by myself and need Your strength, guidance, and wisdom. I surrender all to you as I walk away from the bondage of my past and move forward and forever away from the grip of the pains and wounds of the past. I will pursue and align myself with the purpose You have for me, and my past will not define my path anymore. Help me to trust in You from today on as I work toward my full potential and my destiny, in Jesus's name."

Meditating on God's Word will make you prosperous and give you good success.

> Keep this Book of the Law always on your lips; meditate on it day and night, so that you may be careful to do everything written in it. Then you will be prosperous and successful. (Joshua 1:8 NIV)

God knew He needed to address Joshua's heart, mind, and mouth, and then he could be strong and courageous. Winning the battles in your thought life requires meditating daily on the truths found in the scriptures. The Word is God's truth about you. Be confident in Him and walk in His favor and blessings to your destiny. God gives you the ability to succeed and make wealth, but your mindset must be right. Refuse to be a slave of your outer circumstances. Renew your mind according to Romans 12:2 (NIV):

> Do not conform to the pattern of this world but be transformed by the renewing of your mind. Then you will be able to test and approve what God's will is—his good, pleasing and perfect will.

Being conscious of your thoughts is a great step toward your victory.

> Finally, brothers and sisters, whatever is true, whatever is noble, whatever is right, whatever is pure, whatever is lovely, whatever is admirable, if anything is excellent or praiseworthy, think about such things. Whatever you have learned or received or heard from me, or seen in me put it into practice. And the God of peace will be with you. (Philippians 4:8–9 NIV)

Fill your heart and mind with life-changing biblical truths, always remembering that what you think determines who you are and what you will achieve. You have the mind of Christ. Declare you are blessed and walk to your full potential. In Genesis, we learn about the power of our thoughts and tongue. The people thought they could build a tower to heaven. They saw it in their minds, and then they were able to do it. This is a powerful illustration of the power of our thoughts and words.

> Then they said, "Come, let us build ourselves a city, with a tower that reaches to the heavens, so that we may make a name for ourselves; otherwise, we will be scattered over the face of the whole earth." But the Lord came down to see the city and the tower the people were building. The Lord said, "If as one people speaking the same language, they have begun to do this, then

nothing they plan to do will be impossible for them. (Genesis 11:4–6 NIV)

Proliferating your mental capacity will lead you to achieving your goal. Jabez cried to God to enlarge his territory regarding his worth.

> Jabez cried out to the God of Israel, "Oh, that you would bless me and enlarge my territory! Let your hand be with me, and keep me from harm so that I will be free from pain." And God granted his request. (1 Chronicles 4:10 NIV)

Do not let your limited thoughts hold you captive. Your thoughts determine your destiny. Pray and trust God to give you a greater ability to think big.

You must increase intellectually and increase your worth. Knowledge is power and becomes real when you put it into action. I completed my nursing and midwifery diplomas in Kenya and had planned to complete my bachelor's degree, but family, ministry, and a full-time job always took priority. This was also compounded by our relocation to Texas, but I believed God that one day when my children were older and able to complete their homework without much assistance, I would go back to school and fulfill my desire. In August 2017, after twenty years, I went to university and completed my degree in thirteen months. God honored my hard work and sacrifices, and I graduated with honors. It was a tough time because I was still working full-time. I had church and ministry, and family needed me. My mother fell terminally ill during the same period. I had to travel to Kenya twice in 2018 to take care of my late mother while I continued with my classes. When we pursue God's will in our lives, He makes it easy and gives grace for the course. I remember submitting my assignments at the airports while waiting for my flight. This is because I wanted to intentionally increase my intellectual worth and had to pursue it. There were many barriers and challenges along the path, but I had to battle through them to my breakthrough. I can only say that God is faithful. I'm still on my path to higher glory, trusting in our able God.

Small thinking will limit your achievements. There is creativity in you. Expand your possibilities by thinking outside the box; create it as you see it. Break through every barrier and ask God to download divine strategies to propel you to the next level in ministry, family, finances, and your profession. You must go beyond the borders in Jesus's name.

Whatever surrounds you is critical in your success path and can affect your thoughts and focus. Remove noise, bad influences, clutter, and reminders of the past from your path. Pronounce order in your path as you pray to God to help and guide you. Create your inspirational domain; turn your eyes away from what is worthless. "Turn my eyes away from worthless things; preserve my life according to your word" (Psalm 119:37 NIV).

Align yourself with God's plans and purposes for you. Put no limits on what God can and will do through you. You want opulence? Then create it by an opulent-thinking environment! Think big and detailed. The Lord created you with and for a purpose, and He satisfies you with good things. Work toward your potential. You are an influencer made to leave a legacy for the next generations. Declare you will accomplish that which you were made to do in Jesus's name. Your purpose is great. Pursue it and shine as you glorify God on your path.

You are a chosen generation! You have the power to decree and declare what you want to see in your life. Your words carry power. Declare blessings, greatness, and victory, and you will succeed. Utilize your priesthood authority and decree greatness in your family, marriage, ministry, business, career, and every aspect of your life. Declare you are blessed in the city and outside the city, and through God, you shall eat the good of the land.

> But you are a chosen people, a royal priesthood, a holy nation, God's special possession, that you may declare the praises of him who called you out of darkness into his wonderful light. (1 Peter 2:9 NIV)

When we know our position in God, we shall believe and trust in Him no matter what. Daniel knew his position well, and he glorified God in it. He denied himself and risked his life for the sake of the kingdom of God. God used him to show His mighty power when He saved him in the lions' den. His consistency in faith also made King Darius honor God as a deliverer and a rescuer.

> "I issue a decree that in every part of my kingdom people must fear and reverence the God of Daniel.

> For he is the living God, and he endures forever;
> his kingdom will not be destroyed, his dominion
> will never end, He rescues and he saves; he
> performs signs and wonder in the heavens and on
> the earth. He has rescued Daniel from the power
> of the lions." (Daniel 6:26–27 NIV)

This is a great illustration of someone who understood his position in God and knew he had been called to showcase God's glory through faith and exploits.

When we persist and reach our full potential, God is glorified. The victory path equips us to be used by God like Daniel, and this pleases our God. May the Lord be magnified in your success story. May you live to be an asset and relevant in the kingdom of God and to society.

Myles Monroe said, "You must decide if you are going to rob the world or bless it with the rich, valuable, potent, untapped resources locked away within you."

You are an influencer, loaded with greatness and riches. Make the difference in the family, church, and society, and let your God be glorified.

- Can you visualize the greatness and untapped wealth in you?
- You have the access to it. Pursue it!
- It is your season to manifest and exhibit God's glory.

Declaration

Lord, I declare that through You I have the power for change and prosperity in my mouth. I will command my seasons right and fulfil Your plan concerning me by taking control of my mindset and mouth. There is greatness in me, and I will use every godly strategy and observe every principle and discipline to fulfil Your call and purpose in my life. My life is not a mystery anymore because I now understand You designed me for a great purpose, and You already have my success and fulfilment already planned out in accordance with Jeremiah 29:11. I will observe and adhere to the instructions in Your Word to grow, prosper, and achieve divine victory. I will not fail in my season, and my generations will benefit from my faithfulness and obedience to you, just like Isaac inherited God's promises through Abraham's obedience (Genesis 26:1–6). I am blessed and will be a blessing in Jesus's name.

CHAPTER 7
Stay Connected

The Lord appeared to Isaac and said, "Do not go down to Egypt; live in the land where I tell you to live. Stay in this land for a while, and I will be with you and will bless you. For to you and your descendants I will give all these lands and will confirm the oath I swore to your father Abraham. I will make your descendants as numerous as the stars in the sky and will give them all these lands, and through your offspring all nations on earth will be blessed, because Abraham obeyed me and did everything, I required of him, keeping my commands, my decrees and my instructions." So, Isaac stayed in Gerar.

—Genesis 26:2–6 (NIV)

You have come this far with your progress and success story. Your destiny is sure in the Lord God. Give Him glory and worship Him. As mentioned above, the right connection ensures growth and stability, and fruitfulness is the result. How deeply connected are you with this God who has brought you this far? Are you plugged into Him as your power source? For you to do exploits, you must know your God. In the physical world, if you need your appliances to work, then you must keep them connected to the power source. It is the same in the spiritual realm. For you to continue to grow, experience God's power, and do exploits, you must stay connected to your power source. Put your hope and trust in Him and let Him lead you from one glory to another. God put His divine thoughts and nature within you. Hook up your heart with Him. He is your ultimate source that will never run dry. As long as you have a personal relationship with God, you shall not run out of power and resources.

If you do not have a personal relationship with the Savior, I would like to pray with you.

Please say this prayer and allow Christ to come to your heart today:

"Lord Jesus, I need you today. I confess that I am a sinner and need your forgiveness. I allow you in my heart today. Save and deliver me in Jesus's name. Release your Holy Spirit to guide and walk with me in Jesus's name."

If you have made that prayer, you are now born again. Look for a Spirit-led church and commit yourself to prayer, the Word of

God, and fellowship so that you can flourish in your new life. Keep confessing Christ as your Lord and Savior, and you shall overcome. Your strength in life is in the love that Jesus has for you. Stay connected. Victory is sure in Him. Commit yourself to the church. Learn, grow, and serve God as you understand and pursue your godly purpose.

❖ Daily Keys to Help You Stay Connected

- **Keep God first**

  Giving God a priority enables us to experience His peace in our lives. It is letting God direct your life, which saves you from unnecessary worry. It takes self-discipline to say no to the many distractions in our days. Seek to know more of Him. Obey and trust in Him. In Matthew 6:33, we learn that God wants us to seek things of His kingdom first, and after that, all other benefits will be added to us. The Lord is not limited in His ability and resources. When we put God first, then we shall experience and enjoy His joy, provision, fellowship, goodness, direction, and true fulfillment.

  > But seek first his kingdom and his righteousness, and all these things will be given to you as well. (Matthew 6:33 NIV)

  Love His Word and keep the commandments in your heart. This will prolong your life and bring you peace and prosperity in accordance with Proverbs 3:1–2. Learn to reference the Lord and commit your ways to Him. Do not lean on your own understanding. Submit your ways to Him, and He will establish your path. In 2 Samuel 5:15–17, David inquired of the Lord, and he was able to defeat the Philistines. Inquire of Him daily, and He will direct you on your success path. The Word of God will teach you that nothing is impossible with God. Follow His Word, and you will become what you have always dreamt of being.

> For with God nothing shall be impossible.
> (Luke 1:37 NIV)

- **Be Prayerful**
  Prayer is our core identity. It gives us direction. Through prayer, we invite God to intervene in our situations. It allows us to strengthen our relationship with God. Psalm 145:18 reminds us that the Lord is near to all who call on Him in truth. Prayer is the power that sustains the ability to go beyond your present environment or position. You must guard your prayer life even as you continue with your growth to your destiny. You can be weak today, but when you add prayer, you become a great warrior. Moreover, prayer will release power and blessings from God as well as a breakthrough in your affairs. God's power will burst all the confinements and go before you.

> The prayer of a righteous person is powerful and effective. (James 5:16 NIV)

Seek God diligently. It is through seeking God that we find Him and get to understand His will and His ways. In our seeking place, He washes, prunes, and encounters us, and we grow spiritually. The depth of our hunger for God must surpass all other things because many are seeking Him, but only those who seek Him with the whole of their hearts will find Him. Kingdom seekers are intercessors. They dig deeper for the treasure. Treasures like gold, pearls, and quality fish are not found on the surface or shallow waters. Seek deeper. Listen, and you will hear and find God.

> "You will seek me and find me when you seek me with all your heart." (Jeremiah 29:13 NIV)

If you want God's anointing in your life, you must remain in the secret place. This is your place of intimacy with God. This is where you get encounters and is the source of the anointing and revelations that should drive your ambitions. Give God your all and be desperate for more of Him. Fast to know Him in a deeper measure, and He will reveal Himself to you. His presence transforms and teaches you how to fight right and win on your growth path. When you lose this connection with God, you lose your character. Remain in the secret place, pay the cost, and keep serving God in humility.

Making friends with the Holy Spirit is a must for every Christian. He is our guide, helper, teacher, and counselor. We cannot thrive without letting Him into our lives. When connected with Him, we shall hear His instructions and strategies on how to walk and work, and those instructions will establish us. Stay connected with Him. He will teach you all things.

> "But the Advocate, the Holy Spirit, whom the Father will send in my name, will teach you all things and will remind you of everything I have said to you." (John 14:26 NIV)

- **Have Perseverance and Be Consistent**
  Stay focused and disciplined and diligently obey God. Let not the hurdles on your path derail you. Remain faithful as you serve. Pursue and you shall see God's victory. Sometimes you have to battle through your breakthrough like the persistent widow (Luke 18:1–8). She did not quit. She persisted until she came to her place of power, the place of victory. If the earthly judge could avenge this persistent woman, God promises to avenge you speedily. Keep the faith.

Even when you see only scant evidence on the horizon, keep proclaiming that your victory is at hand and do not quit. Quitting will abort your vision. Keep asking, seeking, and knocking. When we combine the promises of God's Word with a passion to seek Him in prayer, miracles and breakthroughs will happen. Every assignment we are called for requires a breakthrough spirit. There will be opposition because of the ruler of this world, but we have to keep moving. Your persistence will break resistance and yield victory. Develop a mature and strong ability to live with resistance and know that our capacity for breakthrough is in Jesus.

- **Are You Weary of Persistence?**

  Look unto Jesus. He overcame. You will overcome if you do not become weary. He is the author and finisher of your faith. We are called to develop godly qualities that keep us growing from one glory to another. We must make every effort to achieve every quality according to God's Word, and through them, we shall remain effective and fruitful.

  > For this very reason, make every effort to add to your faith goodness; and to goodness, knowledge; and to knowledge, self-control; and to self-control, perseverance; and to perseverance, godliness; and to godliness, mutual affection; and to mutual affection, love. For if you possess these qualities in increasing measure, they will keep you from being ineffective and unproductive in your knowledge of our Lord Jesus Christ. (2 Peter 1:5–8 NIV)

As we continue to thrive, let us remember to keep our eyes fixed on God and His purpose for us and His kingdom.

> Therefore, since we are surrounded by such a great cloud of witnesses, let us throw off everything that hinders and the sin that so easily entangles. And let us run with perseverance the race marked out for us, fixing our eyes on Jesus, the pioneer and perfecter of faith. For the joy set before him he endured the cross, scorning its shame, and sat down at the right hand of the throne of God. Consider him who endured such opposition from sinners, so that you will not grow weary and lose heart. (Hebrews 12:1–3 NIV)

- **Remain Rightly and Tightly Positioned**
  You must be disciplined enough to stay in your position and do what you have been called to do. Build a strong capacity to handle offenses and opposition and keep pushing. When we know who we serve, His position in our lives, and our spiritual position in Him, we should have more faith, confidence, and boldness. Additionally, it should increase the effectiveness of our service to God knowing that we are operating in a position of victory and authority. We must humbly embrace and own the position that God Has graciously given us and serve diligently.

Do not allow the seasons to derail you. Play your role well. Remain active and available. In Genesis 26:2, the Lord spoke to Isaac and told him to stay in Gerar and not to go down to Egypt. Although there was famine, God promised to be with Isaac and bless and establish him. Isaac obeyed, and his life was blessed.

> The man became rich, and his wealth continued to grow until he became very wealthy. (Genesis 26:13 NIV)

As long as you know the Lord is with you, keep pushing and be patient. Your strength must remain big even in the famine. Do not leave your position. Seek God and obey Him. Add patience to your faith and keep trusting in God. We can see God's glory in the famine. Let endurance be built in you. When you persevere, your character is then shaped.

> Not only so, but we also glory in our sufferings, because we know that suffering produces perseverance; perseverance, character; and character, hope. And hope does not put us to shame, because God's love has been poured out into our hearts through the Holy Spirit, who has been given to us. (Romans 5:3–5 NIV)

God will not fail in His plans and purpose for you. Trust in His ability and process. If you are in His will, you will succeed. Be exceptional in your character and defeat every behavioral limitation as you serve. Listen, wait, and humbly serve God in that position. Guard your position with all diligence. Adam was still in the Garden of Eden, but in reality, he was misplaced.

> Then the man and his wife heard the
> sound of the Lord God as he was walking
> in the garden in the cool of the day, and
> they hid from the Lord God among the
> trees of the garden. But the Lord God
> called to the man, "Where are you?"
> (Genesis 3:8–9 NIV)

★ What is pushing you out of your position?

- **Walk in Obedience**
  Obedience is an act of worship that flows from a grateful heart. The Bible says obedience is better than sacrifice.

> Does the Lord delight in burnt offerings
> and sacrifices as much as in obeying the
> Lord? To obey is better than sacrifice,
> and to heed is better than the fat of rams.
> For rebellion is like the sin of divination,
> and arrogance like the evil of idolatry. (1
> Samuel 15:22–23 NIV)

When we obey God, we prove our love for Him and demonstrate our faith in Him. Daniel obeyed God even when it did not seem favorable. Daniel continued with his prayer commitment three times a day regardless of the new law that demanded that everyone pray to King Darius. Daniel did not commit idolatry even in hard times. The Lord he loved, served, and obeyed saved him from the mouth of the lions. The Bible also records that His God was recognized as the Living God, and the king made a new law that everyone was to fear and obey the God of Daniel. Your obedience will be rewarded and will attract God and activate the supernatural power your way. This supernatural power made Daniel successful during the reign of King Darius and Cyrus. If you are willing and obedient, you shall eat the good of the land. This involves both your inward attitude and outward actions. Obey, and God will reward you.

> Then King Darius wrote to all the nations and peoples of every language in all the earth: "May you prosper greatly! "I issue a decree that in every part of my kingdom people must fear and reverence the God of Daniel. "For he is the living God, and he endures forever; his kingdom will not be destroyed his dominion will never end. He rescues and he saves; he performs signs and wonders in the heavens and on the earth. He has rescued Daniel from the power of the lions." So, Daniel prospered during the reign of Darius and the reign of Cyrus the Persian. (Daniel 6:25–28 NIV)

May your obedience be rewarded like Daniel's even as you prosper on your path. Disobedience and rebellion lead to sin and death. Do not miss your breakthrough in your success path due to disobedience. Practice the Word that you have learned and keep your faith in our able God. Let Him be glorified through your obedience and your victory like in the days of Daniel. He is waiting for you to do exploits.

> If you are willing and obedient, you will eat the
> good things of the land; but if you resist and rebel,
> you will be devoured by the sword. For the mouth
> of the Lord has spoken. (Isaiah 1:19–20 NIV)

According to Genesis 1:28 (NIV), God blessed them and said to them, "Be fruitful and increase in number; fill the earth and subdue it. Rule over the fish in the sea and the birds in the sky and over every living creature that moves on the ground." May this be your portion in Jesus's name.

Please pray this prayer with me:

"Heavenly Father, I thank You for how far You have brought me. I now know You created me for a great purpose, and I will fight to accomplish what You made me for. You are the true vine, and I am the branch. I want to remain well connected to You so that I can bear fruits that will last on my prosperity path. Give me grace, Lord, to always put You first, seek You diligently with the whole of my heart, meditate on Your Word, and always serve You faithfully and in humility. I now understand the power of perseverance, and I want to be consistent, relentless, and well positioned in my role in Your service, even as I continue to pursue what You have in store for me. I am not limited because You are great in power, and You are my limit-breaking God. Thank You for Your love and faithfulness this far. I desire more of Your Holy Spirit daily, new encounters, and fresh anointing so that I can impact others around me for Your glory. Thank You, Lord, in Jesus's name. Amen."

It is my sincere hope that this book has been a source of joy and encouragement and an eye-opener, giving you insights and strength. May unspeakable joy flow within you as you arise, pursue, attain, and enjoy that which you were made for. You may have lost all along the path, but the capacity in you is not lost. Roll up your sleeves, put on a victorious mindset, and soar high. You are not limited.

I believe it is your season, and God is together with you. Keep trusting in Him as you humbly serve Him at every level of your success path. He is a God of integrity, and what He Has said He will do, believe in Him. He will do it. He delights in the prosperity of His servants, and you are one of them!

Kindly share this book or purchase a copy for your friend, neighbor, coworker, employee, fellowship group, or family member who has been lost or struggling on their success path. I am sure you will be glad to see them prosper. It can also be very impactful for your Bible study group.

> But blessed is the one who trusts in the Lord, whose confidence is in him. They will be like a tree planted by the water that sends out its roots by the stream. It does not fear when heat comes; its leaves are always green. It has no worries in a year of drought and never fails to bear fruit. (Jeremiah 17:7–8 NIV)

Keep trusting in God and thrive.
You were made to thrive, and you are equipped for it.
God bless you.

Printed in the United States
by Baker & Taylor Publisher Services